Prayers
Manifestos
Bravery

Verity Spott

Pilot Press
London

Trans* Manifestos

To be sure, if I am affected by what does not yet appear to me as a thing, it is because laws, connections, and even structures of meaning govern and condition me. That order, that glance, that voice, that gesture, which enact the law for my frightened body

Here is the third edition of this book. Many of the texts first appeared online at www.twotornhalves.blogspot.com. Versions, drafts and manifestations of the work have appeared in the following publications: Datableed, No Prizes, Materials, Believer and in A Queer Anthology of Rage. A pamphlet entitled 'Trans* Manifestos' was published by Shit Valley. No doubt some of this text has ended up elsewhere. Many thanks to anyone who has circulated the work with or without permission.

This edition is dedicated with love and gratititude to Sean Bonney.

Now, with our senses
                    we've deserted
fulfillment. There's none
                Fit for this love. It sweeps out
in essence, is
 destroyed;
                external wounds.

To begin with the person;
                    such a little life,
                    it seems.
I can barely remember,

        , spoiled.
                    Returning to

hold.

    Falling out from the world

            Tight, it
                assembled. Lips over-
bitten, the horrible vastness of wall.

(Manifesto)

The 'trans community' is as confused as its components. Wrapped in the umbrella narratives of LGBTQ, more narratives are at play within the 'T'. The media organs are obsessed with our bodies, and they want them changed/dismantled/rebuilt/destroyed because they want us to detest them as much as they do. A gross and mawkish preoccupation with gender essentialism leaves a startling war path of bolt down dumb comprehension. I was born in the wrong body is the liberty bell. Dysmorphia/dysphoria dysphorically morphed. It's only a part way saver. It will hurt a hell of a lot. The Metro for beige tolerance. 'Trans*' supposes transition, but where is that transition from and to? Changing gender does not have to mean rebirthing the body. It often does. You should be allowed to tear out its sides, the sides of the law, the walls of the language, the surface of liquid. If you want to change your gender, you can. I think. There's more of an ideological shift involved though. What do you actually mean by gender. What is wrong. The liminal is not the attic space, the bit of left out/limbo/between. No. It's the through space refusing mobility. That is what really fucks up the paradigm. The space that you're supposed to be 'moving' through, toward the blinding sun. Just staying still there. That is the unlimited space. Lock in. The narratives imposed upon the 'trans* community' are as damaging as abject (trans*) phobia because that is exactly what they are. WE SHOULD NOT be attempting a cunning and desperate escape. WE SHOULD BE occupying the space of social discomfort for THEM and not US. Analogical shift from the body to the ground! Who'd have thunk it. We are not in transition. We are in occupation. Internalize any one narration. Make it work. It won't.

(Negating the body, impulsive. Narrative starts from out. Out goes in. In goes out. This process is called 'IMAGINARY' and we think that it probably goes on forever until the final 'other' act which is being completely external. The occupiers were evicted by force. What are they saying? 41% of trans* people commit suicide, the gag statistics).

(manifesto - 2)

Trans*phobia is venom. From the hack of the larynx to the symbolic spew of its semblance. People are stupid like that, aren't they. This violence (all violence) is allowed by, in spite of and because of language - that town, full of lights. Submission, sublimation. This is why there is a lot to be said for a marauding act of subjective violence: Symbolic violence is permanent, the entire artifice of the liberal. Going totally unchecked, ready to fucking waste us. Your death. His report. He will become. Standard, rhyming, multiplicity. Stupid and venomous cohesion. Last night I was told about tolerance. He said that the handiest people in fights round here are the 'poofs'. Do not speak in words. Do not write them. Do not give your children names. No. Invest-in-tolerance... Weak. Speculative rubbish accumulated at the very violent onset of 'normal life'.

I am who I am is a violence.

                        Your enemies say you're 'brave'.

When we speak of 'fluidity'. A block of thought for bridging a rip. That there is a space for movement within the contingent flow of 'general' identity. Does assuming a generality of identity normalise and pacify the unnamable? That's only a question insofar as its treatment at this point. It has no permanence as a question. The answer is yes. Fluidity also supposes a single direction, beginning as rain, tiny droplets, ending in the depths. So the analogy we are creating with the notion of 'fluid' (at least this one) is skewed. It supposes that the identity is primary, and that through its fluid journey, its reckoning, it becomes absorbed into a larger porous and populated mass. The simplistic cache assumption within the analogy of fluid is the set of natural laws governing not only its motion, but its very substance. The inward becomes outward becomes inward becomes outward until the last act of loss. Blissfully ejected into the ether. Or simply entwining one to the other. Or atomizing, the almost infinite. There are a lot of ways of putting it. And putting it off. What is lost within fluidity is the component body and mind. The tiny fleck, its heteroglossia and trembles. I don't know what the answer is except 'yes', or how to resolve it into a meaning. But I keep talking about gender as 'fluid'. And I am starting to think that because I use it so freely and so much that it must be misleading. It is certainly convenient. What I often mean when I say it is that 'gender' describes a lot of small actions, events and patterns; a great many 'behaviours' and visions, icons. These will often shift and alter. So the umbrella of gender is the propensity to shift. But how many of these smaller components create the entire motion? What are their names? Where are they being held? What are the demands for their release? It isn't healthy to think of things like this in terms of anything other than a siege. Can't we get over this paradigm? I mean, from your perspective I might have had quite a nice time being a boy. It's not like being a conservative or something - ahem. Although the majority of them are. They want you to take it seriously. Anyway. I don't have any resolution. Sorry. Fluidity's been doing my head in.

Trans* Manifesto - Revisited.

Paradise/

Those thoughts were some time ago, material thoughts. Ligatures for living. Assessments, like correct protocol & terminology. Glyphs. A false cartography. Now we find ourselves standing at the edge of a horizon, staring over it & back & that horizon is: On the left is a sheer drop, formal. To render oneself as one was: Pick a point in your existence in which you most perfectly enacted the prescribed order of symbols, events, behaviours & motions. Now you can see it stand in it & make it a constant stasis to the exclusion of everything. Exclude pain. Remove pain. Like the horrible contemporary sculptures on the riverbank in Vauxhall. The place of agony is abstracted, not the person, not the people, not the motion but inside the body where all the wrongness lives; a tissue. The second option is to plummet over that edge, imagine it, imagine the surging air. To a point that (it is told to you) is not mapped or permanent, that is fluid, that is fixed. A place called a new body which is separate which is a transplant whereby like jerky you are cured. Vacuumed. Now it is summarised (material truth) that you will stay on the edge. That it is not good to do either thing. Remain where you are or come here. There are no other options. Life...

The reactionary diagnostic process by which trans* people are measured in society at large still does my fucking nut. What it does to that nut is it makes me say 'there was once a point in history where a very reluctant & shame faced medical doctor, probably a man who drank a lot of cheap scotch from small bottles, probably British, probably in his mid fifties, came to the conclusion when comprehending the decomposing life of a queer that this queer had somehow wrongly inhabited its entire universe. That it would have been much better off in one of the neater parallels, & that if only, this doctor thought, it had the nous to ask a doctor, like himself (doctor, lawyer, local councillor, auditor, financial ombudsman etc. etc.) ((& it should be noted this doctor was in fact not a doctor at all but a cheque book ruthlessly attended to in private by a handful of auditors responsible for no precarious labourers)) to cut a long strip from the top of the queers head to the sole of its feet & gently, with forceps, drag its anima sideways through the slit into the air (((for a second here the body is abandoned. Paradise is here, in the abandonment of the body, but not for long because the spirrim once removed from the body is carried))) towards another waiting body with a gaping side & slipped in. The movement from abandonment to habitation takes five years.

Paradise this shit;
                cut in the side of the body head to foot.
      Skeletal split; sew socket. So wrought
     vile cusp,, ideals to body split
                      paranormal. Waist
                      unbecoming.

Ice bath
              split
Ice
              spilt
splint socket
decoder
I-not bodied
              ec
            completely
            ammonia does to eyes
            what I-does to
            body hex
deploy
         r-evan--ent. Genetic impartial
hatch from. Get
            Fixed, queer.

To Resist the (Gender) Binary (trans* manifesto).

Protest is when I say this does not please me.
Resistance is when I ensure what does not please me occurs no more.

To resist is first of all, 1 to never be understood as its own objective meaning 2 resistance reclaimed as a verb 3 an adjective also, to describe the act of a deliberate stopping and when describing the binary 3.1 we must consider a system of deliberate and continued 3.11 sexual exploitation, the grammar of the body, those that would enforce it 3.2 the policing of the self 3.3, 3.4, 3.5 .6 the self 3.7 and that in developing a theory of resistance the primary basis of that theory is its opposite meaning I am / you are / they are in a state of 4 mental illness 5 or ideally bodily wrongness 5.01 pathologists 6 of the sucker 7 of the cunt of the cock 8 of the face and hair 9 of the pupil 10 those same hacks that condemned the habits of collection,, despots of the artery 11 and in that resistance a mesh 12 that I contain no pride means resistance of the language of proudness 13 destroyed as cutting 14 where and when we consider Gender as labour 15 with wages 15.19 but born in the wrong body 15.19.1, but mentally ill 16 cherished of the bitch plea 17 to understand the binary as one would gravity, saturation as a verb, a gravity be done a 18 done thing 19, units of control as helicopters 20 as a comprehensive illness 21 as a natural limit for voting 22 as a body. Understanding resistance as the possible outcome from which natural truth screams back on its back as its back is a snake a 23 uncorseted body. Rotting flesh. Gas. A substance emerged from the natural order,, heated, atonement, never sleep.

The binary enforced in all characters of language, likes. It likes the body (and is like) dead animal, dual carriageway, 4.45pm stiffened && bloated on the curb, mouth smashed, a badger, jaw locked as an A biting the curb. To never sleep. Into exact lines to this mechanic your body 24 two lines across the chest two correspondent ribs damaged Rexam's spinning at 26 points on the social figure of the feminized male given freshly to baying, never sleeping 26 points of the whole remain. The body cut apart the brain touching brain to another brain kissing the shot off hands expulsion of the binary destruction of life = anti life. Blatant hex to walkie panoptic drilling a hole roof mount your coming undone do not explain children in anti livid tetrion 27 mouth spill to a doctored wart. 27.01 do not characterise your children. I can't.

Against Trans* Manifestos

Because I suppose what we've been trying to do so far is establish a language space that deliberately alienates anyone and anything that enforces the gender binary. Pretty simple. Really easy actually; pinpoint every harmonic lie on the map and structurally dismember them. Every word contains at least five. And each five is an enforcement of the perceived two, the double in parallel, one set against the other in a kind of elliptical tragedy that leaves you feeling constantly paralysed. That paralysis, we decided, is stupefaction. It is imposed stupefaction, because if each word in English and in a great many other languages (and sounds, glances, throttles, gestures etc) contains at least five points of false harmony, and each of those five points is contained between two, two harmonic falsities, agh fuck, you get stuck with these five hammering voices barrelling and echoing through your head, you feel dead of them, dead in them,,,,, surrounded,,, agh, lost in an attempt to decipher any vestige of truth whatsoever; confounded by the impossibility laid out by the primal stupidity of language, of bourgeois life and of protocol. Because we feel that, and we cannot understand it, we tend to abandon language. I mean the royal we. So becoming more and more confused by a clammer of desperate stupidity that nobody can relieve you from, you get caught trying to explain yourself over and over again, to your comrades and your enemies; because essentially you are now an example: A stabilising system for those locked in the binary of correct protocol and assurance. That's why so many trans* dialogues have become lodged in a system of correctly assembling language in order to describe the observable.

The observable is describable. That's a material fact. It's not often we'll make that bold a statement, but here we are. The observable is absolutely describable. This is a material fact that cannot be correctly argued against. But that is qualified only when we realise that the observable is tenuous, and the describable is a derivation of the observable, and therefore exponentially tenuous. As the subject (insofar as I am generally observed as a non-invisible member of society) I am exponentially more tenuous than both the observable and the describable, because by the process detailed above I am observed and described. Hence: the visibly trans* subject's general allocation is tenuously derived from two tenuous processes. This is, in part, our constant alienation from the trans* narrative. To play into the hands of the process described above is to draw a map of your life that looks something like this:

Who I am now vs who I was then.
Who I was then vs who I am now.
Who I am now alongside who I was then.
Who I was then alongside who I am now.
Who I am now determined by what I was then
and visa versa. What I am now against what I will be

What I will amount to dispelling the myths
of what I was then, or what I am now, peculiarised
by and into what I will be. As the fuck as
was it will to which the as am you to where as is.

This is only one crude and confused configuration trying to explain and discredit what a trans* manifesto can actually do. I feel if anything things seem to be moving backwards, for our safety. More people are coming towards an understanding, if not a rather clumsy one. The understanding is not what we are, but rather that we perhaps shouldn't be killed. Especially in a liberal country like this, where we might actually have some use. Documentaries, inspirations, Ted Talks. That's a cynical glimpse. Perhaps alongside use there is also the fact of the seam bursting and bursting until it can no longer be contained in what it was once contained by. Thus a larger container. And if you really squeeze your face you'll start to realise how horrible the word 'transition' really is. Determined as it is by a start and a finish, a false double, something that contains at least five harmonic falsities on a liberal map of social reality. Perhaps this is why we have a fetish involving cages; everything impossible to communicate.

Against Transition - A Trans* Manifesto

In total darkness or in a room that is merely devoid of light for hours and hours repeating the same actions over and over again, unable to detach the interior from the exterior, imagining that you were originally hollow: a hollow body waiting for an object or spirit to come and live in that hollow. These are some coping strategies. Over and over again without a shred of light, moving up and down the walls, performing the same abstractions as if they were concrete. It is not that we hate you it is that we have moved away. It is that we question your use of the word 'agency' and 'choice', it is that we can't work out whether your theology is that of Calvin, Arminius or Molina. And we have our own dark night to walk through and we are understandably quite afraid.

*

I spoke to a queer on Sunday. I bent down to rub the spit and grit from their head. They said it isn't out of hatred or even apathy, I'm just not sure I want to come to the altar and watch you and your husband do whatever kind of bizarre ritual it is you're intent upon. Call it my small act of mercy. I screamed at her for hours how frantically you may emulate our disorder how never before have things been so, I snarled, progressive. How you could join yourself to your hip I became very angry and began to spit and kick.

*

We don't have much left to say on these issues. Everyone's been pushed into such shitty counter-rhythms it's basically useless trying to argue. Just this, just remember this, Karen, it isn't a transition it's a fucking apocalypse. So sorry to cause you so much discomfort.

A Hex, on Justice; or Another Trans* Manifesto

I've been thinking about the term "social justice", and about divisions and parting, and about Antiochus IV.

Sometimes things seem to fall into your hands, and it isn't a comfortable feeling. Just like this term "justice", which is chiming in my ears. And thinking of all the magnificent things that are done in the name of justice. The Thompson trial,

Hussein, today, enforced Hellenism, the Patriarchs of Triton, the democratic consistency of the Empires, the harmony of the two genders, the 'two genders' etc. Oh yes, and of course splitting. Principalities. I'm being lost and easy. But there are very few spaces for negotiation. And none of them are safe. If someone tells you that you are entering a safe space they might well be tying a thread around your root around a metal rod and you might just as well put a curse into their face.

The introduction of a safe space has a mirror call it an institution, and you are left there, afraid, and most of the people there are thoroughly kind and good they're going to protect you. Justice, sanctioning container.

> Law, begin a hymn to my god "I don't want allies
> I want accomplices".
> I said when I was hungry;
> Her sandals caught his eyes
>
> her beauty captured his mind
> and the sword slashed his neck.
> And we will equalise our
> we'll horizontal
>
> our. We'll level out the
> enacting justice on our enemies. Child molesters, make a warning,
> abusers, sadists, make a warning, trans*phobes, make a warning, IV?
> A simplified, a limb, those who have not,
> will I be allowed to understand
> you warlords of social justice
> reconfigured tankies and therapists Let all your Creation serve you.
>
> "I don't want allies. I want accomplices".

GENDER DYSPHORIA

I wandered into the room, but there were figures everywhere, on every surface. & so I moved into the outside. Sat on the grass, slept a little. Fell quiet. Saw some figures bobbing. Ducked down into the long grass. Moved across the gap, saw some shadows moving towards me, darted into a hollow, heard them saying things about me. Ducked up into the long grass where I crawled around joyous, came into the house, saw my arms and legs had been covered with burning rashes. Every winter it returns, and I see a room, and in there is a person who could help me with my skin. I am too afraid to enter. I am afraid so I drop down into the long grass and I rest my head and become less and less afraid, and I begin to sleep a little. The itching begins. First it is blissful. The skin breaks. It stings. It begins to weep. It itches again. It is scratched. Blood. Scabs. Scratch. The satisfaction of detachment. And I am terrified that when I enter the room where the kind figure will help to mend my skin or steer me around to avoid whatever it is gets into it,, I worry I'll go into that room and come out with some kind of terrible restraint, and my numbers taken, some kind of diagnosis. I walk out into the sunlight. It is warm. I can see my breath. Everything I can feel or tell by my senses is mistaken. Figures crossing ahead of me, so that the door is the terror. So that I slip into the door where the long grass is reflected and fall into a beautiful sleep. In my dreams you sometimes speak to me. Other people who know you say the same thing. You never speak but in our dreams. This is because of a hierarchy of understanding. I found myself reciting in the long grass as I slowly woke. As I slowly woke in the long grass I found my lips were moving and I was speaking. I found myself reciting: Melancholia, Asperger's Syndrome, Attention Deficit Hyperactivity Disorder, Gender Dysphoria, Prader Willi's Syndrome, Dyspraxia, Slovenliness, Heyfever, Autistic Spectrum Disorder, Dyslexia & Dyscalculia, Anorexia. My eyes were very still fixed on the just moving figures in the hazy distance and my lips were moving over and over again Paranoid Schizophrenia and I was wide awake but very calm as I had learned to meditate on the wild abstractions and leaps of fear this mind does to me. I fell back down and rolled over and stared hard at the room and its window, but over the tall swaying grasses my soft mouth, I caressed my long red hair and touched my lips with my lips and a seam from the bottom of my foot to the top of my head began to gently part, releasing a humming silver light, and with a pair of fingers I caught the edge of the light and gently tugged, and it came sliding out, and I held it there in my fingers, I held her there, and I saw my body lying in the grass, and I held the silver light in my hands as her mouth parted, as she lay there in the grass her mouth parted, and with a sigh she breathed in, and the silver light passed into her body, and she lay there, perfect and sated. I have Gender Dysphoria. With love.

(dispatches)

The year is... uncertain. But this stupid calendar and the light has gone from us. I've been hiding for eight years, much longer; but eight years to the day since I said "I am now hiding". In that time the muscles in our lives have been shocked into torsion. Most people have been sanctioned. Their demotions turned against one another.

If. If I can speak. Speak to you here it is, is merely to confirm what you already know to be true. That we are shrieking, violent and misguided. That we're intent on a nightmare. That we're unified and spoken for.

Something's been happening lately. Meetings. We arrange ourselves into circles and disclose our pronouns, not realising, of course, that this obsession with correct pronouns is a bastard question of protocol, and that it can only serve as a very clumsy transitional demand towards a language which contains no pronouns whatsoever. Perhaps we'll do away with nouns too. A pulse of seismic movements through actions and relations never resting on the reactionary assurance of a specified subject or object. Sure. Dream on, sweaty. Where was I? Ah yes. Protocol:

I've tried not to slander anyone but my head is a fucking disgrace and its been acting up. I forgive you. I forgive you. I'll write again in a month to see if I'm still breathing. I just want you to know that it's all true - all of those suspicions you had. They've brainwashed me; if you'd seen my brain before you'd be glad it had been washed. They're using me to destroy your culture and values. Apparently "only hypocrites are allowed in the Kingdom".

Are you still a sadist? They've weaponised my body. I'm working off my debt through television appearances where I shutdown the free speech of those lifted onto platforms to oppose my life. My existence is mere strategy. Pharmaceutical companies want to accelerate the downfall of civilisation as you know it. They'll destroy gender, the family, daddy's yacht... Oh shit. Someone's coming.
Better memorise all this before they probe me again. Read Gramsci and leave the fraternity.

Something you've suspected. We're all fetishists. Then again I find myself really alienated from what stands around me. That's how you create a new world order; divide and conquer etc, redact your life from the "free marketplace of ideas".

We ate nothing

swallowed the dialogue

...

I've swallowed. Started to fall in cryptics
say all you want is words, say nothing
should be out of bounds I don't buy it I constrict the weight
& messes, unwound the terms of management.

... but imagine being beaten in some
bureaucratic suburban horror, disciplinarian; your body
poised over a beige immaculate carpet; not a character
but there, your softness held in the air

their friends perched on the couches, a florrie of questions
the demeaning synapse in the amphitheatre losing each day
to self worth, abasement; a disclosed property a, a
dismount the signal the petit evils of this suburb

vibrate and flutter deadened and glassless.

Now consider being farmed, the farmer and feeder explains it's not you, not your pain, nor you who are there and neither is there a farm. It's typical snowflake hyperbole - the electric pulse to the udder the meat grinder rolling. Try not to exaggerate, speak nicely, take your calcium.

Dear Jonny,

funny I mentioned taking calcium. I've been having two tablets a day for a couple of months now; didn't really know why I was taking them. Then this weekend I managed to break a couple of ribs. It's terrible. I can barely even work on my manuscript and washing my hair takes a whole twenty five minutes. I was wondering if you could ask the Arts Centre to wire me over a couple of grand and arrange a flight out to Jersey and a hotel - that one near the coast with the delicious fruit breakfast and the Keith Richards Bar. I feel the air would do me a lot of good and once I'm recovered I can drop off the latest stats re: minority representation for funding applications in the next quarter. You'll all be the first to know. I think you're going to shit a brick!

Yours, in Grace and Recovery,

I confess.

I'm so tired of seeing what ought to be a sensible adult debate degenerating into name calling and babyish slobber. For a while I've felt completely alienated from both sides of this conversation (there are two sides, Karen) but I'm beginning to feel more and more that the gender identity politics (POLICE more like! Eh?) that claim to support me are selling me short and in fact to some extent erasing my subjectivity. I'm taking a deep breath here because I'm probably going to be torn to pieces but it's time to blow the lid off this whole project once and for all. I am a trans man. I used to be a lesbian woman but was encouraged to transition because of the way I enacted my gender. You will have been told that the process of transition is long, painful and arduous. It's in fact so effortless it's basically nothing. Like walking into the t o i l e t. Well, it was certainly arduous but what they won't tell you is that it can happen very quickly. I was referred to one of the "unofficial" gender clinics (there's at least one of these in every county hiding in plain site with the outward appearance of a normal doctor's surgery) and within a couple of years I was a man in thought and deed. At first I was happy to get on with my life as a bloke, and things were quite stable. This all changed when some friends introduced me to Miriam, a woman who I soon began to fall in love with. It turned out that Miriam was a trans woman. I took her to meet my family and they sealed our lives with their magnanimous approval. Readers I got married to her. We were approached by the BBC to be in a documentary about trans lives and under some pressure I agreed. We received an enormous payment to be part of the accompanying campaign and received subsequent direct payments from the BBC and a company whose name I won't mention here for fear of recriminations, but I will state that they produce certain medicines and have a calculated net worth in the billions, and that the umbrella private equity fund that presides over said company incorporates companies that manufacture the likes of over the counter toothpastes, soy products and certain corners of our social media - I hope this gives you an idea of where this is going.

The campaign and documentary the BBC had launched stated its aim as "raising awareness of the issues and struggles faced by transgender people in society". Let me tell you, it did that and then some. Once the project had finished a private debrief was arranged with some head honchos from the Beeb. We were told to speak to nobody about the meeting. Even here on this shadow account and under an assumed name I feel the Boleyn's axeblade of a threatening observers eyes hovering above the back of my quivering neck. At the meeting we were thanked for our work and told that if we continued to campaign with the BBC in accordance with the directives of the aforementioned company we would never need to work again. Having lived in the ankle of our overdrafts for all of the years we'd been together we readily agreed and signed a contract which consigned our lives to our future course.

A week later we found ourselves in a hall near a hamlet called Brig O' Doone in Scotland. We entered a hall. A plaque resided at the end of the cavernous space that read:

'The only philosophy which can be responsibly practised in face of despair is the attempt to contemplate all things as they would present themselves from the standpoint of redemption. Knowledge has no light but that shed on the world by redemption: all else is reconstruction, mere technique. Perspectives must be fashioned that displace and estrange the world, reveal it to be, with its rifts and crevices, as indigent and distorted as it will appear one day in the messianic light. To gain such perspectives without velleity or violence, entirely from the felt contact with its objects – this alone is the task of thought.'

I later learned that this was a quotation from the philosopher Theodor Adorno who's work (along with other Frankfurt School philosophers) we set about studying in rigid harmony for weeks on end. Throughout this time we were fed an almost entirely soy based diet and encouraged to brush our teeth with high fluoride concentration toothpaste at least six times a day. Our resolve to spread the agenda our identities had bestowed on us solidified in our minds like a pyroclastic bomb in an iceberg of nitrogen. We left that place hellbent on immanentizing the Cultural Marxist eschaton. My wife and I were seperated to pursue our ends where the company saw fit and it is here you find me working as a blogs and content editor at Mumsnet (which, by the way, is not a safe place for discourse around these issues).

This last letter just about scratches the surface of what's really going on. Let me spell it out for you and risk my own neck in the process. This is a heist. The BBC is beholden to large pharmaceutical giants who are controlling huge aspects of what you see and hear and trying to impose a Cultural Marxist new world regime one world government that will entirely abolish traditional gender roles as we know them - further, they seek to transform the human body beyond its current form and make the entire population infertile. The next stage; well, who knows? I am stuck here for now but will release more dispatches if I can. If you don't hear from me again in three months call the Roberts. Keep fighting the good fight, but proceed with caution. Remember, all of your clumsy Orwell references and Handmaid's Tale cosplays are being noted down under "LEGITIMATE THREATS". Get any trace of fluoride out of your house, cover your webcams and be sure to use a proxy server at all times. You heard it here first. The GRA was an inside job.

"I Never Said that I was Brave"

The title of this text is the title of a song by mewithoutYou which can be heard on the album 'A-B Life'. The intermittent quotations are from the same song.

I.

I never said I was a "real woman" nor did I adhere to your distinctions - the broken knotted world of your categories and gibbets - your essential primacy. Nor did I frivolously saunter here without being drenched in steaming tar - in alienations, agonies and abuses.

Nor did I attempt to rupture your spaces. Nor did I shepherd my body and thoughts into a singular character.

Nor did I assume the dialectic and character of your history. Oh, essential subject.

Nor did I claim the keys to the apparatus of an entirely dismantled ideology.

Nor did I sleep through the night, nor said I was fully awake - those were your claims - you inhabited them and threw them at my body, assumed my history. I did not say that I was brave but I did say that I was beaten in the Men's Room, in the road, but I also said that I was afraid and I also dragged my feet and I also screamed for the deracination of established sex.

We were stockaded, doubled up and gagged then made to speak.

I was lucky and neither was I lucky. I did not ask to be taken into a medical examination, to be a pathologised subject, a piece of transferable data some kind of stabilised example.

Yes, perhaps there were moments of asking to drop out of the universe. There were pleas against the force of stabilised gender norms, but then there were still more pathologists and shitheads and explanations forced into our mouths and our eyes and people throwing around words like "toxic" and "drag" in the indistinct daylight there were mouths crying out against our ideologised bodies so we lurked in the toilets like the filth we were.

And yes, sometimes I do hide there waiting for silence before I can show my face and yes it is a weaponised generality that speaks inside it.

I never asked to join the U.S. Marine Corps. I was party to the mutiny by proxy of thought, there was a derangement of conflicted motions and love was taken out of us.

I did not give my consent to the idea of an opposite, to a world of stupefied duality: That under the Gender Recognition Act 2004 individuals may change their legal sex but require approval from the medical profession, a diagnosis of gender dysphoria and to live as a member of the opposite sex for two years, of who was to conduct this analysis - which upstanding professional with preordained certainty, and what great liberties might be achieved after the tests and cures, the prescriptions and siphons.

Ahead of you is a perfect sequence of rational and professionally state sanctioned grills, routers and sieves. Behind you is a repressed derangement of habitation. Inside you, a screaming barb of lyric, passion, expression and defiance. Now sit tight for the probe. "I never said that I was brave."

II.

There are some quite complicated social equations.

A wish to abolish gender. The subject that destabilises the binary.
The natural fallacy

In the middle of that equation is the subject, the lyric "I". This character will be made to continually testify. They will be hounded by the wish to deconstruct and the ideologies of natural gender. Both of them at once. Hate crimes against trans* people. Natural women. Alpha males. Radicals. It is not possible to merely live. They must live to testify. Their visibility will be their act of martyrdom. Or try this: You live in a political situation where you have been told the laws of civility. At the same time things that you do in your day to day life have direct links to the torture and murder of people you will never look at. You have been told what is a democratic decision. You have never chosen a form of governance. You have been told what a debate is. You have spoken with corpses in your mouth. Until that is understood there is not a unit of sense in any single schema. "I did not mean any harm" does not equate to "I did no harm". We are harm. To most of the globe we embody it, pronounce it. We are the enemies of the soil we stand on. Then there are the circumstances of day to day living. Do you ever feel you are being watched? No. Embodying harm does not mean you can justify feeling guilty. Guilt is the fascist inside you cackling. There is no movement from point one to point two. There is an entropic motion of spheres perhaps but you are not hanging off a hook and this won't get you off. Nobody likes to be interrogated. Yet here we are put on the slab for your discussions. Men are still at large. The way they win is imagine the natural fallacy and the wish to abolish gender abolishing instead their intrinsic contradictions and acting as an agent of death against the subjects who dare to dissolve parts of their taught genders. You are now an agent of that violence. It's like every kind of splitting. The desire for unity is tantamount in some situations to the desire for the death of the other. They were taking photographs to send to the estranged families of people who are, what do they say? 70% more likely to consider or commit suicide. They called this the "documenting of a reasonable debate". I cannot write about these people in clear language because they will doxx me. Before you begin to say the word "reasonable" consider the power relations. "There is only one way out", they thought as they balanced on the edge of the bridge. There is no radical movement in enforced binaries. There is no psychedelic plane in the enforcement of motionlessness. Sometimes someone says something to you that makes you want to die. That is not an abstract metaphor. We were sitting by the window. Neither is it a logical set of circumstances. The enemies of the soil do not get to speak with logical voices. They howl in the wind. They do not possess the powers of reason. There is an argument to be made for removing the bodies inside our brains piece by piece. Apart from that "I am afraid". "I do not mean harm" when "I know not what speaking is" or "I do not know what I mean" or "creating a world devoid of context". It will end with a few horrible men wandering around in the dark screaming "faggot!", "you deserve death!": All of the walls will be gone. There will be nothing left to echo. They will be stamping on bodies and dead soil. They will beg their own shadows to take offence.

III.

> (*You might sleep, but you'll never dream*
> *Onward! Progress! Or so it seems*
> *And you might laugh, but you'll never smile*
> *Come on in and waste away awhile*)

It was hard to get to sleep last night. I was drunk and tired. I took myself home, took myself into my bed and lay there. There were sounds and expressions going back and forth through my head, through the air. I'd read every word you had written. I had tried to listen to it. There was a pit of despair in my stomach.

The body lay there. It had no words. The words do not exist. Everything is loaded. I bind you to love yourself. I bind you to your immaculate care. From doing harm to others. From doing harm to yourself.

The questions have lived in my body. They are my body. It lives underneath a microscope - in its self hatred and wrecked determinism. Its visibility is its own worst enemy. It was not put here for you - it was not put here against you. It was beaten. It was hidden. It was not an object of compassion. It broke under eyes. There were walls of eyes.

It never wished to become a theory. It never intended to hurt you. It had its life inside it forever. It kept it at bay. It never tried to stop you from speaking, even when your words were nails. Every movement it made - every sign, was the production of a question. It had you in its dreams.

It saw a small act of law as a tiny emancipation. Though it knew that the law was the enemy the law made a tiny but significant change and the body felt a tiny weight lift up. The law was in the air, under the ground, in our mouths and our hearts. No matter what we did it would hound us, bury us, coerce us.

> (*When dreams of rings of flowers fade and blur*
> *Giving way to that familiar ill*
> *Come over and part your soft white curtains*
> *Where I'm waiting for you still*)

It remembered how well dressed the moralists were when they opened the doors of the town hall and said "people of Austria, our identity is under threat." "Men of America, if you don't make a stand you will lose your jobs and your wives". These are the words of the custodians of law. They said "we need to have a fair and reasoned debate about the primal identity. They are a threat to our primacy. They are trying to infiltrate our spaces. They are unsafe."

They said "womenfolk, your essence is under attack". All the while they enforced the binding essence of women. They constrained women. They used their bodies against their bodies. They said "you are under threat." All the while those custodians of law were the threat. All the while the mind of the abuser was left unquestioned.

Bodies like this one became the icon of threat. They became abstract examples - they were subjunctive bodies. They were used to demonstrate what the custodians of the law might be allowing. They were made to be hypothetical. But listen, dear friend, listen to our weaponised bodies. Listen how they howl, how they are mocked and disassembled. Our bodies are united in their strategic capacities. I bind the law. I bind you, law. I bind you against causing harm to others. I bind you, law. I bind you to cause harm only to yourself.

And then you shocked me. You took a picture of a human being up onto a pedestal. You made an example of a human in pain. You questioned the fabrics of a human identity. A cold argument. Asked for a logical dissemination. I didn't think you could do that - become a custodian of the law. What would that spirit say? That immaculate compassion - the one who has seen into your heart beyond the tracts of laws and of bodies and of polarities. What would its words be? What would it make of these establishments of fixed icons? How will the spirit purge you into love? It was a coldness I had not heard in your heart before. I bind your heart against the cold.

The custodians of law threw wide the doors of the town hall. They set out the rules of engagement. They guided the voices of the people. Steered them away from their compassion. They taught their tongues to articulate their displeasure. They showed each other to the targets. They held up bodies in front of the people and said "these bodies are a threat". They said "these bodies are mentally ill". No one thought at this point about how the mentally ill should be treated. Their resolve became firm. The custodians of law said "these bodies want you to be silent. Look how they scream when we try to debate. See how their eyes are filled with hatred!"

> (*My stomach swears there's comfort there*
> *In the warmth of the blankets on your bed*
> *My stomach's always been a liar*
> *I'll believe it's lies again*)

Did you look into those eyes? Did you see what fear looks like? Did you really see hatred? "See how they do not want you to speak?" screamed the law, all the while the law kept the women in their seats, in their bridles. All the while the coercion of voices raged and hissed. The bodies on the platform were ready to take leave of this world. All the while the law whispered in the ears of the people. All the while the men looked on. All the while I bind you against the law, against coercion, against the formation of fixed polarities. All the while the bodies on the pedestal trembled and said "I bind you" through the dust in their mouths.

The bodies were photographed and examined. Their names were passed around. The discussion was the end of compassion. The law dismantled it. The law enforced and switched. The law crept into houses. I bind you to your love. I bind you against definition. I have no power. I do not exist.

The bodies in the air, their sound: "I do not exist. I do not exist. I do not exist. Only you exist. Only you exist. I do not exist." And the law fizzed, its subjunctive electricity. The spirit. The law. The sky. The body. The water. The fire. The wind. The chaos of the silent air.

(My Lord, how long to sing this song?
And my Lord, how much more of this pretending to be strong?
When she stands before your throne
Dressed in beauty not her own
All soft and small, you'll hear her call)

Last Manifesto

How hateful you've become. It's the day before the deadline for the GRA consultation. Maybe you're reading this in a few years time and you don't know what that is - you don't know what anything is. The whole world has been sucked out and paralysed and you're not capable of knowing anything. No. That's now. Hostile subject, you don't know anything at all. We are left with almost nothing. Hatred is not knowledge, it is idiot passion. It burns in me. The reason this feels strange is because I barely know what any of it means anymore. It feels like they're having another one of their elections which have collapsed onto us over and over again. Even a few years ago where that desperate little optimism called Labour made a bit of headway. Everything that's happened in electoral politics for the last ten years has been a hideous repulsive disgusting ridicule of human subjectivity. Actually, twenty years, actually, more or less forever, and more or less almost nothing. And so here I am in a horrible state not dressed yet, working away at the thing that occupies every minute of my entire life and often takes me closer to universal central point, making me worse, being told by my financial ombudsman (I don't know what that is) that I am not working and that I need to be working, and I look at social media where loads of gorgeous people are doing their absolute best to accommodate people who are like me, or a bit like me, or not at all like me, or a little bit to the right if you squint but almost like me or who are almost nothing like I am or who are nothing like you and I also are, or who are a bit more than almost nothing, or who are almost nothing like almost nothing, asking things like "how can I be a good ally?". I don't know what this is. A nebulous vocoder. Fuck you, ally. You are as bad as rotten soil. That's not even an insult. I am the thing rotting in the soil and you are the soil. "You are my dust" I read somewhere. It's not even going to accumulate into some wonderful moment if it goes well, the GRA if reformed as proposed will at best attempt to save a few hundred lives and what are a few hundred lives now when we are almost less than nearly nothing, after all of this? How hateful I've become. It happens from time to time. I try to resist and curtail it but it's so difficult. To have seen magnificent humans brimming with love deliberately fall out of this world and to have even a vague understanding of the mechanisms that seem to be sustaining it against so many incredible possibilities - rendering the better good utterly impossible, it's hard not to recourse to hatred... It's been a couple of hours since I wrote that. Now I'm a little calm. Or exhausted. The thing about this moment - the thing, is that it's one of those questions that I can't believe we're even asking. Around that questions is a swarm of grieving fear being clutched tightly in the fists by opinion journalists and people who've been thrashing against us obsessively for years. Suddenly they're walking under the banner of "legitimate concern". We just want the noise to stop. That's all I can hope for at the moment. I'm sick of human lives being at the centre of violent questioning. I'm sick of your pretend intellectualism. I'm sick of your stirring. There is no such thing as a trans poetics. I'm sick of the great big old world keeps on turning. There is a tongue in the neck. There is rotting soil. Moments of collective healing. What. Slow death.

(niner - after Nat Raha, after Linus Slug)

Slow death, now as in gently they made
        a centre, this hazing remedy
        hostility recognition act
        legitimized until no moving;
slow death, slow death, slow gridded death, by
        what. How hateful you've, no not "hateful"
        exactly more like a gentle grind
        called love, exactly. What. Reduced us
to releasing wasps in their houses.

Today is the last day in the entire world. Waiting at the end of something for almost nothing. Waiting at the end of something that is also nearly nothing for almost nothing to happen. Being attacked for nothing and for wanting nothing more than nearly nothing, for wanting almost nothing more to happen. Being killed for being almost nothing at all. Being nothing. Being almost something, nearly the idea of something but almost called nothing. Waiting at the end of nothing for almost nothing to achieve almost nothing; we are almost nothing waiting for almost nothing for an amount of time that feels like just a little more than almost nothing but is in fact barely anything, and is nearly almost nothing. Feeling almost nearly nothing about waiting for almost nothing being killed for almost very nearly nothing nothing and almost feeling nothing. Being feelingly crushed under the weight of almost nothing knowing nothing forward and nothing backward, knowing that 'forward' and 'backward' is less than almost nothing, the inescapable less than nearly almost nothing whose consensus we are stretched inside to the length of nearly nothing. The consensus of being almost nothing for almost no time, for feeling almost everything knowing that everything we are always feeling is slightly short of almost nothing. You are everything to me, and it feels like we are somehow going to be crushed again, gently crushed to the glint of a scent of a flavour of a speck of a maddeningly tiny almost nearly nothing, a miniscule almost nearly nothing coerced and tendered into a world of minute almost nothings forever, an objective and administrable, almost nothing. an objective and administrable slow and silent death.

Published in the U.K. by Pilot Press

First edition published in 2018
Second edition published in 2020
This edition published in 2023

© 2018 Verity Spott
All rights reserved

Cover by Richard Porter

Printed on 100% recycled paper

ISBN 978-1-7393649-5-3